بسم الله الرحمن الرحيم

In the name of Allah, the most Gracious, the most Merciful.

We encourage you to review this book with your child before they start coloring. Your child will learn a lot about what Muslims do during the holy month of Ramadan thanks to this.

Assist your child in using the 30-day planner to track their growth during this wonderful month.

رمضان كريم

This Ramadan coloring book belongs to

_____

Ramadan is the 9th month of the Muslim's Calander.
It begins with the sighting of the new moon.

Ramadan lasts for 29 or 30 days, with the celebration of EID-UL-FITR marking the end of Ramadan.

Ramadan Kareem

1	2	3	4	5	6
7	8	9	10	11	12
13	14	15	16	17	18
19	20	21	22	23	24
25	26	27	*Eid Mubarak*		
28	29	30			

The fasting day starts with Muslims waking up early to eat Suhoor (breakfast) before the sun rises. Suhoor with the family is always fun.

Muslims pray their 5 daily prayers throughout the day starting with Fajr, Dhuhur, ASR, Magrib and Isha.

It is also recommended to make lots of Duas throughout the day so Allah will be pleased with you.

RAMADAN KAREEM

The Quran was revealed to Prophet Muhammad (PBUH) in the month of Ramadan. It is good to recite the Quran often in Ramadan. Allah will reward you.

Muslims break their fast at sunset with Iftaar (dinner). This is a wonderful time with the family.

Having Iftaar at the Mosque is even more fun!

After the Isha prayer, Muslims also offer extra prayers so Allah may be pleased with them. Taraweeh is one of these prayers done during the month of Ramadan.

It is quite enjoyable to pray Taraweeh at the Mosque with loved ones.

Muslims also enjoy making extra Dhikr, Duas, and reciting the Quran when at the Mosque...

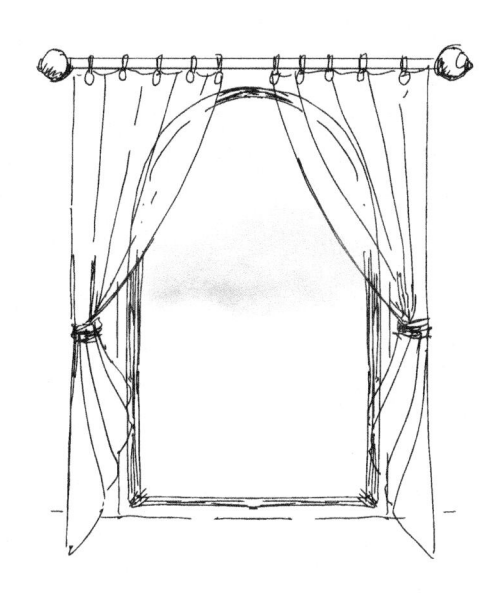

and at home.

ALLAH LOVES ME

Muslims help those in need by giving them food and supplies so that everyone can have a nice Iftaar and Suhoor.

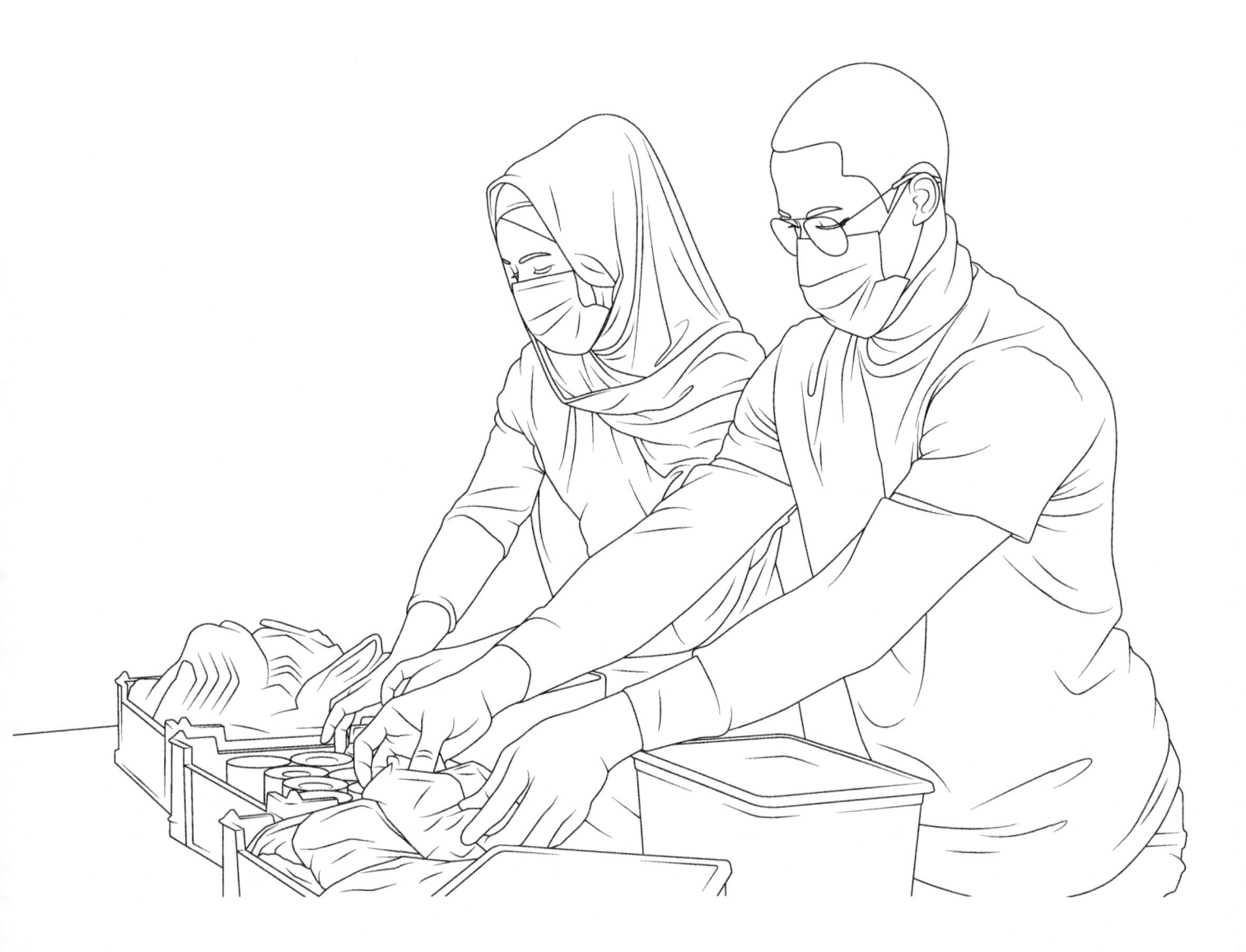

Providing grains to those less fortunate so their parents can cook delicious meals as well.

Muslims must also donate a certain percentage of their wealth to charity. It is called zakat.

The ending of Ramadan is marked with
the sighting of the new moon.

EID-UL-FITR

It is a joyful and festive time. On the morning of Eid, Muslims visit the mosque to offer the Eid prayer.

EID-UL-FITR
They celebrate the EID festival with family and other Muslims..

EID-UL-FITR
Muslims also exchange gifts on EID day!

EID-UL-FITR
And have lots of delicious food with family and friends!

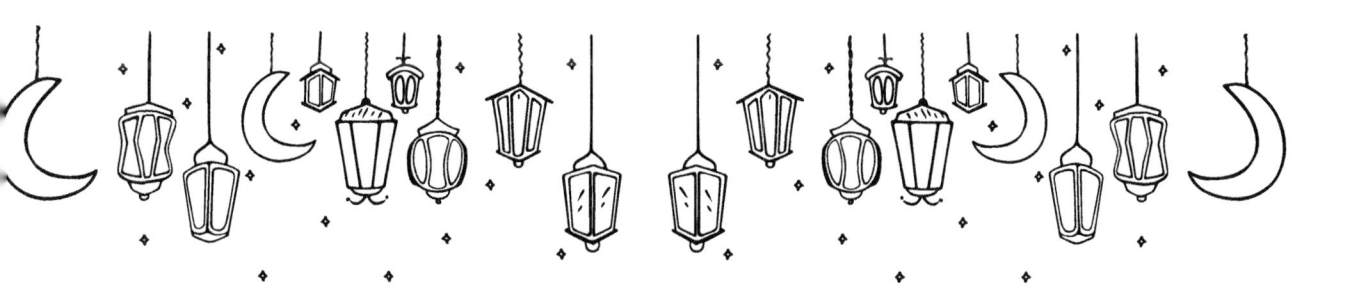

Ramadan KAREEM

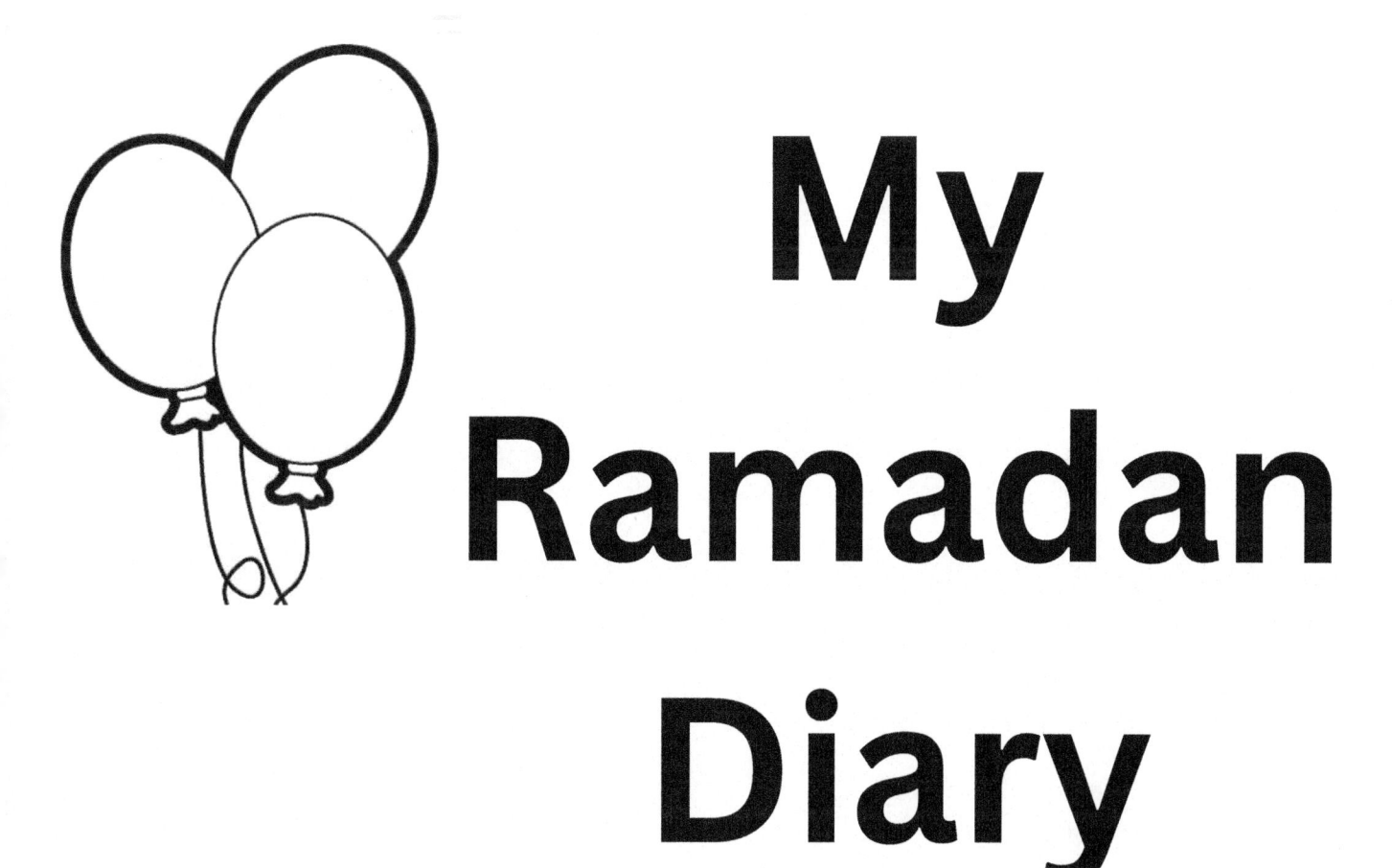

My Ramadan Diary

Note: You should fill out the additional "good deeds" section at the bottom of each page....

Ramadan: Day 1

Today I,

- ☐ Fast
- ☐ Pray
- ☐ Make Dua
- ☐ Recite Quran

And, my other good deeds today are:.

☆

☆ ☆

☆ ☆ ☆

Ramadan: Day 2

Today I,

- ☐ Fast
- ☐ Pray
- ☐ Make Dua
- ☐ Recite Quran

And, my other good deeds today are:.

☆

☆ ☆

☆ ☆ ☆

Ramadan: Day 3

Today I,

- [ ] Fast
- [ ] Pray
- [ ] Make Dua
- [ ] Recite Quran

And, my other good deeds today are:.

☆

☆ ☆

☆ ☆ ☆

Ramadan: Day 4

Today I,

- ☐ Fast
- ☐ Pray
- ☐ Make Dua
- ☐ Recite Quran

And, my other good deeds today are:.

☆

☆ ☆

☆ ☆ ☆

Ramadan: Day 5

Today I,

- ☐ Fast
- ☐ Pray
- ☐ Make Dua
- ☐ Recite Quran

And, my other good deeds today are:.

☆

☆ ☆

☆ ☆ ☆

Ramadan: Day 6

Today I,

- ☐ Fast
- ☐ Pray
- ☐ Make Dua
- ☐ Recite Quran

And, my other good deeds today are:.

☆

☆ ☆

☆ ☆ ☆

Ramadan: Day 7

Today I,

- ☐ Fast
- ☐ Pray
- ☐ Make Dua
- ☐ Recite Quran

And, my other good deeds today are:.

☆

☆ ☆

☆ ☆ ☆

Ramadan: Day 8

Today I,

- ☐ Fast
- ☐ Pray
- ☐ Make Dua
- ☐ Recite Quran

And, my other good deeds today are:.

☆

☆ ☆

☆ ☆ ☆

Ramadan: Day 9

Today I,

- ☐ Fast
- ☐ Pray
- ☐ Make Dua
- ☐ Recite Quran

And, my other good deeds today are:.

☆

☆ ☆

☆ ☆ ☆

Ramadan: Day 10

Today I,

- ☐ Fast
- ☐ Pray
- ☐ Make Dua
- ☐ Recite Quran

And, my other good deeds today are:.

☆

☆ ☆

☆ ☆ ☆

Ramadan: Day 11

Today I,

- ☐ Fast
- ☐ Pray
- ☐ Make Dua
- ☐ Recite Quran

And, my other good deeds today are:.

☆

☆ ☆

☆ ☆ ☆

Ramadan: Day 12

Today I,

- ☐ Fast
- ☐ Pray
- ☐ Make Dua
- ☐ Recite Quran

And, my other good deeds today are:.

☆

☆ ☆

☆ ☆ ☆

Ramadan: Day 13

Today I,

- ☐ Fast
- ☐ Pray
- ☐ Make Dua
- ☐ Recite Quran

And, my other good deeds today are:.

☆

☆ ☆

☆ ☆ ☆

Ramadan: Day 14

Today I,

- [ ] Fast
- [ ] Pray
- [ ] Make Dua
- [ ] Recite Quran

And, my other good deeds today are:.

☆

☆ ☆

☆ ☆ ☆

Ramadan: Day 15

Today I,

- ☐ Fast
- ☐ Pray
- ☐ Make Dua
- ☐ Recite Quran

And, my other good deeds today are:.

☆

☆ ☆

☆ ☆ ☆

Ramadan: Day 16

Today I,

- ☐ Fast
- ☐ Pray
- ☐ Make Dua
- ☐ Recite Quran

And, my other good deeds today are:.

☆

☆ ☆

☆ ☆ ☆

Ramadan: Day 17

Today I,

- ☐ Fast
- ☐ Pray
- ☐ Make Dua
- ☐ Recite Quran

And, my other good deeds today are:.

☆

☆ ☆

☆ ☆ ☆

Ramadan: Day 18

Today I,

- [ ] Fast
- [ ] Pray
- [ ] Make Dua
- [ ] Recite Quran

And, my other good deeds today are:.

☆

☆ ☆

☆ ☆ ☆

Ramadan: Day 19

Today I,

- ☐ Fast
- ☐ Pray
- ☐ Make Dua
- ☐ Recite Quran

And, my other good deeds today are:.

☆

☆ ☆

☆ ☆ ☆

Ramadan: Day 20

Today I,

- ☐ Fast
- ☐ Pray
- ☐ Make Dua
- ☐ Recite Quran

And, my other good deeds today are:.

☆

☆ ☆

☆ ☆ ☆

Ramadan: Day 21

Today I,

- ☐ Fast
- ☐ Pray
- ☐ Make Dua
- ☐ Recite Quran

And, my other good deeds today are:.

☆

☆ ☆

☆ ☆ ☆

Ramadan: Day 22

Today I,

- ☐ Fast
- ☐ Pray
- ☐ Make Dua
- ☐ Recite Quran

And, my other good deeds today are:.

☆

☆ ☆

☆ ☆ ☆

Ramadan: Day 23

Today I,

- ☐ Fast
- ☐ Pray
- ☐ Make Dua
- ☐ Recite Quran

And, my other good deeds today are:.

☆

☆ ☆

☆ ☆ ☆

Ramadan: Day 24

Today I,

- ☐ Fast
- ☐ Pray
- ☐ Make Dua
- ☐ Recite Quran

And, my other good deeds today are:.

☆

☆ ☆

☆ ☆ ☆

Ramadan: Day 25

Today I,

- ☐ Fast
- ☐ Pray
- ☐ Make Dua
- ☐ Recite Quran

And, my other good deeds today are:.

☆

☆ ☆

☆ ☆ ☆

Ramadan: Day 26

Today I,

- ☐ Fast
- ☐ Pray
- ☐ Make Dua
- ☐ Recite Quran

And, my other good deeds today are:.

☆

☆ ☆

☆ ☆ ☆

Ramadan: Day 27

Today I,

- ☐ Fast
- ☐ Pray
- ☐ Make Dua
- ☐ Recite Quran

And, my other good deeds today are:.

☆

☆ ☆

☆ ☆ ☆

Ramadan: Day 28

Today I,

- ☐ Fast
- ☐ Pray
- ☐ Make Dua
- ☐ Recite Quran

And, my other good deeds today are:.

☆

☆ ☆

☆ ☆ ☆

Ramadan: Day 29

Today I,

- ☐ Fast
- ☐ Pray
- ☐ Make Dua
- ☐ Recite Quran

And, my other good deeds today are:.

☆

☆ ☆

☆ ☆ ☆

Ramadan: Day 30

Today I,

- ☐ Fast
- ☐ Pray
- ☐ Make Dua
- ☐ Recite Quran

And, my other good deeds today are:.

☆

☆ ☆

☆ ☆ ☆

Printed in Great Britain
by Amazon